PRESERVING GREATNESS, STEWARDING PURPOSE

A Daily Propulsion Towards Intentional Living

Neisha A. Sibley

Preserving Greatness, Stewarding Purpose: A Daily Propulsion Towards Intentional Living.

ISBN:

979-8-9905441-0-9 (paperback)

979-8-9905441-1-6 (e-book)

Foreword

Whilst I recognize the abundance of written materials existing that focus on purpose, I must give due credence to this addition to the collection. Truthfully, I will admit to the fact that the matter of purpose cannot be over-emphasized, underrated and certainly cannot be allowed to become extinct. As such, I have found this book, "Preserving Greatness; Stewarding Purpose: A Daily Propulsion Towards Intentional Living" to be a timely and critical resource to be added to one's library and made use of in one's life. It is a useful tool to have if one is to sharpen one's vision toward understanding and fulfilling the ultimate meaning of life. As the title suggests, the book will seek to daily hold the hands of the readers as they pass through the dark tunnel of obscurity in life and propel them into the light of purpose's actualization. As a purpose-advocate and one who is a bi-product of stewarding purpose, I am encouraging you to read this book as it seeks to help you on your own journey to preserving the greatness that is in you.

I have had the opportunity of meeting, interacting and serving with Neisha Sibley for the past five (5) years and I have quietly admired her uniquely subtle but aggressive pursuit of purpose in her own life. On many occasions, she could be seen, heard and felt demonstrating this critical life quest through her involvement in the performing arts ministry, through her passionately vocalized conversations and expressions as well as through the audacious writings from her first publication. Consistently, Neisha has demonstrated that she understands that there was more to the life God has given her and that despite the odds she faced, she was bent on finding that more, fueling that more and finishing that more. Neisha, is a woman who preserved her greatness, stewarded her purpose and is daily seeking to fulfill her God-sealed mandate on Earth.

With her creativity and laughable tones and expressions, the author, Neisha, seeks to engage us as her readers with the truth and weight of her writings in a persuasive and relatable manner.

This resourceful material also includes many reflective questions and real-life and applicable analogies that make the concept of preserving greatness and stewarding purpose very easy for readers to appreciate and understand. With topics such as "You are GREATNESS", "Don't Expect Them To Understand" and "The Isolation: Shh, Not

Yet" from the chapters, Neisha naturally lights a spark of interest in the minds of her readers about how they ought to pace and brace themselves on their path to preserving and stewarding their purpose and greatness. With a substantial recognition of and partnership with the value of words, Neisha brings this book to a close by sealing it off with a series of daily affirmations and declarations for her readers to be guided by as they position themselves to be propelled into their God-given positions.

Neisha is chronically aware that there are many persons who are living below and outside of their heavenly standards and mandates on Earth; many are living without greatness and without their purpose. Through her writings in this book, she aims to capture as many minds and spirits and to lead them to learn the truth about who God has made them to be and to help them to navigate through the corridors of greatness. Her desire is for readers and hearers of her message to be propelled to live an intentional life of greatness and I am in no doubt that it will do just that for you and more. Accessing this book provides an opportunity for you to contribute to your future and to leave a legacy for generations behind you. I implore you therefore, to be intentional about your pursuits of purpose; invest in your life by accessing a priceless copy of this book.

Melicha J. Smith

Author|| Speaker|| Prayer Advocate|| Motivator

Table of Content

DEDICATION

I dedicate this book to every son and daughter of God who wants to take their lives to another level in God. This book is for those who know that there is more on the inside of them but may be afraid to tap into it. It is for that individual who has been sidetracked by life's demands and has ignored the promptings of the Holy Spirit to launch out into the deep and attack their goals and dreams. Additionally, this book is for those who are ready to abandon the old ways of thinking and cultivate a new mentality that will propel them to live with intentionality.

ACKNOWLEDGEMENT

Most importantly, I want to thank God for giving me the ability to pen another book. I also wish to extend my utmost gratitude to Prophet Dr Joseph Mwenya (Author of *Holes in the Ground*), Mrs. Melicha Smith (Author of *Prayer For A Struggling Warrior*), and my sister/friend, Mrs. Gizel Carter (Author of *Road to Salvation*), for their words of encouragement, prayers and guidance throughout the writing process. Finally, I want to thank Prophetess Shanique Shand-Johnson and her amazing publishing team for assisting with various components of the publishing process. Heaven bless you all.

INTRODUCTION

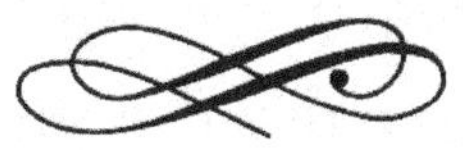

What have you done with your life thus far? How have you been managing the gifts and talents that God has given to you? On average, how much of your time is spent fulfilling the goals of friends, families or bosses versus fulfilling the goals and dreams that God has given to you? If your response to these questions were all favorable, then it means you are on track, but if they are not, it means you have some work to do.

God has purposefully equipped you to do great things. What He has given to you are not just random thoughts and ideas. You were created with a God-sealed mandate specifically assigned for you to carry out. Though life may get busy at times, as a steward, it is your responsibility to carefully manage the gifts and talents given to you because God will hold you accountable. You may not have to answer to God in this present moment, but you will have to give an account someday. The only thing that separates now and eternity is *time*. So, what will you do with your time? No excuses will be accepted then. No excuses will be beneficial then. The privilege you have now is to make the best of your time by doing what God has called you to do, and today is a great day to start. All that you need to fulfill your God-given mandate has already been given to you; you just need to discover it. There is no doubt that you were born to be great and to do great things. In fact, the God that you serve is a GREAT God, and since you are an heir of His kingdom, you already possess the seed of greatness.

It was molecular biologist and medical researcher Oswald Avery who in 1944 discovered that DNA transmits heredity. Geneticist Maclyn McCarty who was also a part of Avery's discovery, referred to DNA as being the 'material of inheritance'. This is quite an interesting description because the Bible tells us in Romans 8:17 that we are indeed co-heirs or co-'inheritors' with Christ Jesus. This means we have the privilege through Christ Jesus to partake of the greatness from our eternal benefactor—God, who made us eternal beneficiaries. I believe that those born of Christ have spiritual genes coded with the letters G.R.E.A.T within them. Therefore, it is important that we preserve this greatness on our lives at all cost. For us to manifest greatness, we must first believe it. While manifestation will not take place by solely believing, your belief plays a crucial role in the process. After believing what the Word of God says about you, you will undoubtedly be motivated to preserve the greatness on your life, which is what this book is about.

The word preservation is oftentimes misused or misunderstood. Preservation is not solely safe-keeping, but it is also protecting the content and value of something of high quality in order to sustain its durability and functionality. When food scientists add preservatives to food, it is to ensure it stays fresh and in good condition free from all microbes or contaminants that could possibly make it bad. According to Science Direct, preservatives are added to foods to prevent it from deterioration, enzymes and microorganisms. Two of the most common preservatives are potassium sorbate and ascorbic acid. If you were to inspect the ingredients in your food, you would see the word *'sorbate'* on most of them. This is because potassium sorbate helps to inhibit the growth of yeast, mold, and fungi. By stopping the growth of these organisms, potassium sorbate prolongs the shelf life of the food. Like food, there are valuable qualities within us that should be preserved from any microorganism in our environment that could potentially deteriorate, spoil or reduce the shelf life of our gifts and abilities.

Preservation prolongs longevity; it creates a hedge of protection around things we deem valuable. Noone preserves something that is detrimental to their life and well-being. Once we realize the value of something and how much it can be of benefit to us, our natural reaction is to protect it and keep it close. This is how we should approach greatness. All of us were created to be great, to do great things, and to be known among the great. Afterall, our heavenly father is great and He calls us to be like Him. One of the things I have noticed in my life over the years is that many people tend to be intimidated by my ambition and sometimes classify it as pride or haughtiness. Many times I have had to wrestle internally with the magnitude of thoughts bombarding my mind while having to contend with my environment that repeatedly bellows, "It's too big of a dream; it won't work!" I have tried thinking small on many occasions but my attempts failed every time. Mediocrity and I could not cohabitate although I tried. Time confirmed that we were indeed mutually exclusive. Having discovered this, I made up my mind that I would never shrink to fit in because I was born to stand out anyway.

Today, so many people have walked away from their true purpose because they allow the voices from their environment to live rent-free in their minds, slowly diluting the once concentrated vision that

God has placed within them. Though many of us fall victim to this, the awakening truth is that no one can do what God has called you to do like you can.

Yes, there are many preachers, teachers, singers, leaders but only you can preach, teach, sing and lead the way that God has created you to. God has put that burden or desire in your heart for a purpose. He gave the vision to you, not your environment. Whether your environment is your parent, spouse, best friend, relative, boss or other person of influence, the reason they may not be able to see the vision and feel as passionate about it as you are, is because they were not the ones God placed the burden on; you were. He created a problem specifically for you to solve: You carry the solution within you.

Dream Killers vs Constructive Critics

In the process of answering the call to greatness, we will need a strong and godly support system. We all need people who are honest, loyal and as driven as we are. We need people around us who are committed and can hold us accountable. But did you know that there is a difference between those who offer constructive criticisms and those whose assignment is to kill your dreams? Dream killers are those who open themselves up to be used as instruments of the enemy. Dream killers sometimes disguise themselves as those who have our best interest at heart, supposedly giving 'constructive criticism' when in reality their goal is to deter, discourage or thwart you from the path of greatness. However, constructive critics are those who give actionable feedback to help you improve by suggesting ways to amplify your idea to make it bigger than what you initially imagined. A dream killer attacks your goal and questions your ability to achieve it, while a constructive critic highlights room for improvement while supporting you through it. We should ask God for the Spirit of discernment so that we do not confuse the two. Those who support our dreams are those who we should keep around us. Think about it... It is already hard work to keep believing that this gigantic goal of yours will be achieved, so how much more of a task will it be to harbor negative-minded people around you too? Who you need are people who can help you believe. They are the ones who the Lord will raise up to stand as a strong, positive support system who will see the dream through to fruition.

Do Not Shrink

The greatness placed upon us by God should not be downplayed or ignored. Rather, it should be protected, nurtured, developed. When we preserve greatness, we automatically stand against anything that will want to corrupt the purity of our calling, mission and mandate. Overtime, we discover the things and people who are in alignment with preserving our greatness so we know who we should keep around us. There are people in the world today who are called to be great but you would never know it because their current situation does not align with the word God spoke over them before they were born. What we sometimes forget is that our mandate was created before we came into existence. God did not create us without first preparing the path. The late Dr. Myles Munroe was well known for saying that the wealthiest place on Earth is the cemetery because so many people have died without fulfilling their God-given purposes. There are so many books that were not written, songs that were not sung, and businesses that were not launched because those in the graveyard died before accomplishing them. You cannot afford to be one of those who die with all their treasures inside.

Do Not Live Below Your Potential

Many people today are living a lesser life—a life that God did not plan for them to live. This can be as a result of laziness, ignorance or the works of wickedness. The enemy has always been trying to hijack our future to keep us from becoming who God has ordained us to be. It is painful to see mentally ill people eating from the garbage, not because they want to but because they are not aware of what they are doing. This is a common way in which the enemy attacks those born with the seed of greatness. He knows that if he attacks the mind of an individual, it will affect their overall functioning because the mind is the Central Processing Unit (CPU) of the body. If we are to ever walk into the level of greatness that the Lord has called us to, we will have to protect our minds at all cost. A practical way to do so is to pray over our minds by declaring the word of God over ourselves each day. Though the enemy may try to attack different areas of our lives, we do not have to fall victim to his attacks. There are ways that we can rise and dominate like we were created to. This book was strategically written as a spiritual manual to help you navigate the corridors of greatness. It is my desire that at the end of your reading you will be propelled to live an intentional life of greatness.

CHAPTER 1:

YOU ARE GREATNESS

"Now the Lord had said unto Abram, Get thee out of thy country, and from thy kindred, and from thy father's house, unto a land that I will shew thee: And I will make thee a GREAT nation, and make thy name GREAT; and thou shalt be a blessing." (Genesis 12:1-2, KJV)

The call to be great was extended to us from our very inception. Abram, whose name was later changed to Abraham, was the father of all nations. The Lord had made a covenant with Abram. Now, it is said that a covenant is a binding contract or obligation between two people. In Genesis 17:2-4, the Lord made known the covenant to Abram: ***"And I will make my covenant between me and thee, and will multiply thee exceedingly. And Abram fell on his***

face; and God talked with him, saying, "As for me behold my covenant is with thee, and thou shalt be a father of many nations."
So far, we see that this covenant has different parts to it. The covenant made to Abram was not a sole promise. The Lord had many different levels for which he wanted to make Abraham GREAT and one of the most significant ways to do so as seen in Genesis 17:5 was to change Abram's name. This is what verse 5 says:

"Neither shall thy name any more be called Abram, but thy name shall be Abraham; for a father of many nations have I made thee." (Gen 17:5, KJV).

For God to multiply Abram, he needed a new identity. This man was selected to be the father of generations to come. If there was going to be a generation with a new identity and new purpose that would capture the revelation of the GREATNESS within them, it would be the generation that comes from Abraham's lineage. Therefore, it was incumbent on Abraham to lead the charge. This decision was not determined by Abraham, it was God who decided to give him a new identity. In verses 6-8 of Genesis 17, the Lord specified ways in which Abraham was going to be great, some of which included producing kings, and making the covenant an everlasting one by extending it to generations after his and his children's children. He was promised the inheritance of lands and assured that in all of it, He would still be their God. It was Abraham's obedience that landed him those blessings, of which we are inheritors today. It is critical that we understand the power of being identified by a new name. Abram's name change further underscores that the Lord will not make you GREAT without giving you a new identity.

“Therefore if any man be in Christ, he is a new creature: old things are passed away; behold, all things are become new.” (2 Cor 5:17, KJV)

A few ways in which the Lord changes our names include changing our marital statuses, giving us revelation of the spiritual meaning of our name, breaking curses attached to our names or giving us a completely different name which may require a deed poll. Could God not have blessed Abram without changing his name? Sure He could, but we serve a God who does all things new (2 Cor 5:17). In this verse, Paul tells us that those who have accepted Christ have officially transitioned from the old to the new. The Bible specifically refers to this person as a ‘new creation’. In addition, Isaiah 43:18-19 tells us that in order for God to do a ‘new thing’ we have to get rid of the old ways of thinking.

> ***"Remember ye not the former things, neither consider the things of old. Behold I do a new thing: now it shall spring forth; shall ye not know it? I will even make a way in the wilderness, and rivers in the desert." (Isaiah 43:18-19, KJV)***

The God that we serve is a God who upgrades us, transforms us and makes us new. In addition, Matthew 9:16-17 shows us that God is always ready to do something new. His response to John the Baptist was that it is not comely for someone to put new wine in old wineskins or sew new pieces of cloth onto an old garment. It takes a transformed mind to think this particular way because we live in a world where quick fixes and fast attainments are desirable. These are not the result of a mindset of greatness. The transformed mind that has come into the revelation of the greatness it possesses will understand that integrous attainment takes time and discipline to be achieved. Anyone who wants to produce 'new clothing' in a fast and cost-effective way may think of sewing new pieces of cloth onto an old garment but it takes an individual who is intentional about their end goal, reputation and integrity, to pursue something completely new. Greatness is not trying to replicate the life of someone else. Greatness has to be revealed, beheld, imparted to you. You just cannot conjure up a feeling of greatness some days and then it subsides when you don't feel like it. Greatness, though given to us from the beginning, has to be specifically revealed to you through intimate time with God. This is because though we are all called to be great, we have different areas in which we will manifest that greatness.

In the book of Judges Chapter 6:12, we see this revelation given to Gideon by an angel of the Lord. All throughout Gideon's life, he felt as though he was the least in his family. Gideon had never seen anyone in his family being considered for any major projects or leadership tasks. As a result, what the angel said to Gideon baffled him because he had never thought about himself as a leader. He did not foresee it in his future, and he sure had not witnessed it in his past. However, what an admirable posture Gideon soon adapted! Though he was aware of his family's history of being insignificant and poor, Gideon did not hesitate to align himself after receiving the revelation of the greatness on the inside of Him. Like most men of God in the Bible, Gideon asked for a sign and after seeing that sign, Gideon quickly prepared himself to take on the role to fulfill the mandate given to him. He made sure to build an altar as an emblem of the covenant of God's peace and called the name of that place 'Jehovah Shalom'.

Isn't it funny the ways in which God works? As human beings, we are socialized to believe that people who are opponents in battle are those who are properly trained to fight or persons from influential backgrounds, but this was not the case for Gideon since he was the 'least' in his family. However, the Lord defied human logic and Gideon (whose name actually means' mighty warrior') was summoned to battle. Did Gideon have the slightest idea of his potential? Probably he did, probably not. From the language of the text, it echoes the idea that Gideon had not thought of himself or anyone in his family as being great. This should encourage us to not count ourselves out based on our perceived inadequacies. The Lord can call forth greatness to come alive within you when you least expect it. When the Lord reveals to you who you truly are, it is important that you respond correctly. If for any reason you have unconsciously disqualified yourself from being used in great ways, it is time for you to address those areas of disqualification so that you won't end up rejecting the call of greatness. In verse 15-16 of Judges 6, Gideon challenged the angel to confirm the instructions through a sign, instead of perpetuating the point about the insignificance of his family. Perhaps Gideon did this because he at least wanted some form of confirmation that this was indeed from the Lord before openly rejecting what could be his destiny.

In contrast to Gideon's posture, we see the consequences of those who disqualified themselves from the call of greatness and had to reap the consequences of their actions. In Luke 1:20, Zechariah the Priest, openly rejected the call of greatness by his disbelief. Instead of believing or even asking for a sign as confirmation, he quickly disqualified himself on the premise of being too old for childbearing to even be possible. This should not be our posture. The God that we serve is one who specializes in impossibilities. Therefore, when He commands us to do that which seems impossible, we should be encouraged that He is the one who will strengthen and enable us to do it. One of the main reasons why many people subject themselves to less than greatness is because they are intimidated by the magnitude of that which they are called to do. This should not be your narrative. Even the root word of greatness; 'great', suggests something grand. How can we expect to walk in greatness without having grand encounters, grand ideas, grand problems that will require a great mind to solve? Great people normally carry a burden for something. This is not just any burden, but it is a strong desire to bring justice to something, to birth or invent something that will create a solution for something. This burden is what will propel your actions to solve that particular problem. This burden will not dissipate until you have taken the steps to solve that problem, and even then, it won't be quelled until you have successfully completed it.

One way to identify your purpose is to ask yourself some of these questions: "What has been bothering me every time I see it, hear it, taste it, smell it? Is this thing a bother to others too? What are the ways to alleviate this discomfort and introduce an advanced level of comfort to myself and others by extension?"

Do not become comfortable in discomfort for the call of greatness awaits your timely response.

> ***"Four young men from Judah—Daniel, Hananiah, Mishael, and Azariah—were among those selected. The head of the palace staff gave them Babylonian names: Daniel was named Belteshazzar, Hananiah was named Shadrach, Mishael was named Meshach, Azariah was named Abednego. But Daniel determined that he would not defile himself by eating the king's food or drinking his wine, so he asked the head of the palace staff to exempt him from the royal diet." (Daniel 1:6-10, MSG)***

Daniel was called to be great but he was not born in a castle or a palace. In fact, Daniel was a Jewish boy who was taken into captivity by Nebuchadnezzar. Though he was not born in a palace, his gift made room for him to serve in the king's palace. When we harness our greatness, the Lord will promote us. The Lord will put us in places for us to use our gifts for His glory. One of the most noble and admirable qualities of Daniel was seen in his courageousness even when he was faced with life-threatening situations. Daniel had an unshakable confidence in His God. He understood that preserving greatness meant for him to be integrous, not tampering with the purity of his calling, mission or Godly mandate. Though the king's food may have looked attractive and smelled amazing, awakening all the senses of his appetite, Daniel was more focused on protecting that which he was called to do and be, and that was to be great. One of the things that the Lord will do is to test our commitment and integrity to the call of greatness. Daniel could have given in but he was disciplined. He could not trade this invaluable gift for a buffet of food that would have defiled his greatness and possibly corrupt the freshness of his gift.

Though Daniel was ridiculed, he remained steadfast and committed to the things of God. Many around him may have wondered what could have possibly caused a young man to employ such discipline knowing he is just a youth, but Daniel was called to be great, and this greatness was revealed to him so he could not ignore it to indulge in what everyone else was indulging in. Because of Daniel's unshakable faith, the king's men gave him a challenge by trying to convince him that he would be weak at the end of the challenge and as a result, he wouldn't be selected by the king. Nothing could be further from the truth. In the natural world, it would make every sense for someone who was just feeding on vegetables and water to lack strength compared to others who are eating all the different meats and proteins. Because of his wisdom, Daniel knew this was not merely a natural act; it was more spiritual than the king's men could imagine. At the end of the challenge, the God who Daniel obeyed, showed up and proved that He is the preserver of life and the promoter of men. Daniel came out looking healthier and stronger than those who ate the king's meat. This story helps us to understand that when we remain obedient to God even in the face of authority figures, He will show up and work on our behalf. Daniel's unyielding attitude throughout the book would always precede his victories.

When you are called to be great, you have to believe it. By his actions, we can see that Daniel was overly persuaded that the great God who lives within him was far more powerful than a human who had assumed worldly royalty. It is important to note that Daniel was not disrespectful to his earthly leaders. However, he was more submitted to the King of kings, Jehovah God Himself.

We live in a world today where some Christians at some point have tried to please others who are not submitted to God, and in trying to please them, ended up displeasing their God instead. It is injudicious to expect earthly leaders who serve other gods to understand our spiritual dispositions. They will never understand unless they have proof that our God is truly God. Daniel did not waste words trying to convince them that his God was going to come through for him and they were just wasting their time and resources. Instead, he remained faithful and obedient to God, knowing that obedience is a love-language to Jehovah God. We should seek to adopt some of these principles and postures. In essence, Daniel knew that he was called to be great and so instead of trying to convince men, he allowed the orchestrator of Greatness to speak through His wonders to them.

It has been debated that the men to women ratio in the Bible suggests that it was a very patriarchal time. However, this does not negate the fact that those women who were selected to be a part of this great book possessed greatness. One of these women was Queen Esther. Esther was a class act. Humility, wisdom, beauty, grace, elegance were just a few qualities she embodied. Esther, though an orphan, did not allow her limitations to stop her from manifesting greatness. Instead of the limitations causing a hindrance, it actually propelled her into greatness. Her route to greatness was not achieved independently. Esther had the help of her faithful cousin, Mordecai, who was adamant that something great would come from her story. It is important to note that we can either look at our limitations as reasons for constant failures, or we can see them as motivation to manifest the greatness within us. Esther's obedience to run for Queen was met with God's favor. This was powerful because sometimes we complain that we don't have the help we need to get to where we want to when we haven't even taken the first step. I believe when we yield to obeying God, He will send the help that we need. Of all the 400 virgins who were competing for the royal position, Esther (a Jewish Orphan girl) was selected to be Queen.

Rest assured, God knows where you are. He knows how limited your resources are but He wants you to exert faith so He can take you to the next level. God would have already provided Hegai to show Esther immense favor and ordered seven maids to see about the needs of Esther throughout her preparation process. Esther's greatness did not stop at her becoming queen. In fact, that was the genesis of her greatness. Like others who had their names changed as a part of their call to greatness. Esther's previous name 'Hadassah' was changed to conceal her identity but would later be revealed because greatness cannot be hidden. What started off as positional greatness quickly transitioned into a heroic act that ultimately preserved the lives of other great people. Esther was reminded by Mordecai during a time of impending anguish, that her position as queen was not merely for show but was rather a strategic position at a pivotal time when Jewish lives were dependent on her immediate response.

Nothing that we go through, whether losses or successes are solely for our good.

It is also for the good of others. If we lose, it is so that we can learn what not to do, so we can ultimately win, and when we win, we get to teach others how to win. Esther could have responded selfishly, but wisdom would have enlightened her that if Jewish lives were being threatened, that included her life too. An immediate response was requested by her cousin Mordecai, so an immediate response was what Esther gave. Knowing that fasting and prayer are powerful tools to use when seeking the face of God, Esther did not hesitate to call a fast, and while she was in her palace praying and seeking the face of God, so were the other Jews. What happened next was a powerful response from God. When we seek God in spirit and truth, it is important that we become open to His response. Many times, we seek God for an answer, but we already have a preconceived expectation. Instead, we should go before Him with an open mind so that when He responds we do not get terrified about His answer. After the fast, Esther felt led to confront the King without an appointment, something that was very dangerous to do. However, her response was "If I perish, I perish." This powerful posture does not only speak volume of Esther's selflessness but also her heroism. Heroes are those who risk their lives to save others, and Esther did no less. Esther was truly a great heroine in the Bible.

As mentioned earlier, great people are called to solve a problem and Esther solved the problem the Jews were confronted with. The tragic plot to assassinate the Jews was cleverly twisted to save their lives.

If you sense that God has called you to manifest greatness in a certain area, be vigilant for the call will come with risk-taking, problem-solving and possibly 'lives-saving'. It may take some sleepless nights too, but that's what great people do. We have to be willing to burn the midnight oil while everyone else is busy sleeping on their destinies.

The Heights by Great Men

-Henry Longfellow

"The heights by great men reached and kept were not attained by sudden flight, but they while their companions slept, were toiling upward in the night."

CHAPTER 2:

DON'T EXPECT THEM TO UNDERSTAND

"And Joseph dreamed a dream, and he told it to his brethren: and they hated him yet the more." (Genesis 37:5, KJV)

Understanding who you are and what you carry is paramount to preserving greatness and stewarding purpose. However, expecting everyone to understand who you are and what you carry is a recipe for disaster. The truth is, everyone is at a different level of growth and maturity in their lives; whether it is in their Christian walk or outside of Christendom. One of the mistakes we make is to think that everyone knows what we carry and is excited to see it come to fruition. Most of the people around us either don't understand the vision, don't think we can accomplish such a vision, or don't even have a vision for themselves to begin with, hence they cannot envision or even support your vision. Since God is the one who gave you the vision, it is important that you ask Him to connect you with like-minded visionaries.

Joseph was called to be a great leader, but his brothers did not understand this. I believe Joseph himself did not understand the magnitude of greatness he had within him in the initial moment. It was this greatness that caused all of the problems Joseph later encountered. What Joseph knew was that he was different, he did not like the same things others liked, and he was not driven by what drove others. He knew his dreams were strangely deep and they resonated with his spirit. He also knew that his father loved him very much. What Joseph did not know was that the sparse feeling of greatness he initially sensed was far greater than a literal expression of his family bowing down to him.

The greatness on his life positioned him as a government overseer for a whole nation. Though he was thrown into a pit, it was a perfect position for him to be sold into his purpose. Yes, Joseph was *sold* into purpose. What started out as betrayal became his transition into the palace. Joseph's brothers could only see their action as an opportunity to get rid of him, but God saw it as the channel that would transport Joseph to where he needed to be. Their resentment against Joseph served a purpose.

For this reason, we should not always count a negative situation as 'doom and gloom' because it could be the very method God uses to position us into our purposes.

Like Joseph, I too had my fair share of family ordeals to deal with. I cannot say that I forgave them immediately. It took me well over 2 years to bury the hatchet and come to a place where I could speak about the event without feeling tension against them. Today, I write about it not to lament but to rejoice because what others meant for evil, God turned it around for my good.

One of the things that we must understand is that we can be the hindrance to our own progress. One of the ways we do so is to harbor unforgiveness in our hearts. When I weighed the burden of unforgiveness and the weight of my purpose, I had to make a decision to relieve myself of unforgiveness. This is because the weight of the glory on my life is far more valuable than carrying a burden I was not meant to carry in the first place. Though it was not easy for me to let go, I did, and so can you. Today, I encourage you to do the same. Examine your own life to see if there is anything that could possibly hold you back from becoming all that God has called you to be. Holding on will hold you down, but letting go will let you grow. You will soar, you will elevate, and you will rise when you let go and let God. Today, you should make a concerted effort to let go of anything that could stand in the way of your next level in God. Had Joseph not forgiven his brothers, he would not have been able to serve them the way he did. Yes, he broke down and cried when he saw them but his tears were not tears of pain; his tears were a sum of his emotions.

> ***"And Joseph made haste; for his bowels did yearn upon his brother: and he sought where to weep; and he entered into his chamber, and wept there." (Gen 43:30, KJV).***

He felt so much joy from seeing them again. Joseph was even more relieved to learn that his father was still alive. The love he had for his brothers did not lessen over the years. Instead, his love for them grew stronger. Their absence from Joseph's life certainly made his heart grow fonder towards them. This is a lesson that God is capable of changing the condition of our heart towards those who may have wronged us. He will remove negative emotions and give us positive ones when we submit them all to Him.

Beautiful Redirections

Over the years, I experienced many disappointments in the working industry whereby I was treated unfairly by those in authority who were abusing their power; it went as far as them terminating me because they were not fond of me. However, in retrospect, there was always a beautiful redirection. The short experiences I had while working at a Jamaican restaurant and at the Preschool, both of which I was terminated from, gave me all the experience I needed to start my own businesses. Both experiences were necessary for me to hear the complaints of consumers, see the gaps in management and experience toxic workplace culture that needed to be changed. These prompted me to create mitigation plans for my very own businesses so that those problems would not be named among them. Today, I am the proud owner and operator of Faithouse Foods, a faith-based food establishment currently operating as a bakery, and The Anointed Math Tutor, an online-based math tutoring program created to assist K-5th grade students. This is not to imply that God is going to give you businesses in the industries that rejected you. While it is possible for God to do so, this example is just to encourage and remind you that God does not waste experiences. He will sometimes make you uncomfortable to get your attention. He will even cause others to reject you to redirect you to where you need to be.

A typical work environment includes the employer, employees, and then consumers on the other end. One of the limitations that exists is that a typical worker does not have much say in the decision-making process of the company since most workplaces have a centralized decision-making system. If you have experienced job termination or any disappointment in the place where you thought your purpose was, do not be dismayed. What may look like a disappointment to you may be a beautiful redirection in disguise.

As the creative that you are, your ability to transform someone's workplace is limited by the amount of room they give you to do so. If the Lord has called you to the marketplace to operate successful businesses, you will not find much satisfaction working for people, until you yield to God's direction for your life. God has placed so many great business ideas within us but many times we think the ideas are there to help improve the workplaces that we are currently in. While it is totally possible for the Lord to give us a vision to help improve the work environment that we are a part of, the truth still remains that many of us are lagging behind in toxic workplaces trying to ascend professionally when the Lord wants us to take the leap and start our own businesses. There are people out there who dread getting up in the morning because their work environments are unhealthy, in every sense of the word. Yet they get up each morning and drag themselves there because they do not have another source of income if they should resign. This is an unhappy and unhealthy way to live. I do not believe this is what God wants for His children.

If you are reading this book and this is your reality, let me use this opportunity to inform you that your source of income is on the inside of you, you only need to tap into it. The longer you sit in those unhealthy workplaces expecting things to magically change or for management to see your potential and promote you, the longer you will suffer from their toxicity.

Management may not see you as the treasure that you are, but it is for you to know how valuable you are and act upon it. I am sure those who terminated me did not understand the treasure they had in their presence. They did not understand the greatness within me but it was not for them to understand anyway. Sometimes we waste time trying to get others to be as convinced about our vision as we are when they are not the ones to whom God gave the vision.

Do Not Allow The Enemy To Play Mind Games On You.

The enemy has a way of discouraging people by telling them that their plans won't work or that there are many people with similar ideas. However, similar does not equal the same. This means that though others may have similar ideas, they are not the same as yours because you have a unique level of creativity to contribute that will make your idea stand out from the crowd. What you do with the idea is what will result in your sense of fulfillment. Some people ignore the ideas and subject themselves to toxic working environments for years and as soon as they fall ill, they are replaced in an instant. Sometimes they do not even receive a 'get well' card from their places of work or a phone call to check on their progress.

There are so many people who are unhappy in their workplaces today, because every year they anticipate getting promoted and it never happens. In fact, I was privileged to speak with a young lady who told me she built someone's company from the ground up. She spent over a decade building up this company but did not find any satisfaction there in the end and so she left. Now, understand that this was not her own company. She was one of the first set of employees there and with the knowledge that she had, she went above and beyond to get clients for the owner who never truly knew how to honor her. This situation reveals that this young lady is very gifted and has what it takes to start her own company. Judging from the outcome, it is easy to think that she wasted a decade of her life, but it can also be seen as a learning experience for her and exposure to that business industry.

God does not waste experiences; He has a way of disrupting our routines to get our attention. Sometimes God has us in a place for a season and a specific reason, but He will allow us to go so far and no further. In the end, He will cause both the good and the bad to work out for our good. Do not allow people's ignorance of your purpose to cause you to be ignorant of your own purpose. Let them be the only ones who are clueless about who you are. Stay focused.

> ***"And Eliab his eldest brother heard when he spake unto the men; and Eliab's anger was kindled against David, and he said, Why camest thou down hither? and with whom hast thou left those few sheep in the wilderness? I know thy pride, and the naughtiness of thine heart; for thou art come down***

that thou mightest see the battle." (1 Samuel 17: 28, KJV).

From the above scripture, it is clear that David's brothers were unaware as to who David was and what he was carrying. David's brothers did not think much of him but that did not stop God from anointing him as king. David was heavily anointed and versely trained to do battle. He was a young king but his brothers only saw him as a sheep-keeper. David's brothers refused to see his vision. They chose instead to see David as someone who wanted to compete with their acclaimed valor which would soon prove deficient in the face of a giant on the other side of the battle. The questions David asked prior to 1 Samuel 17 verse 28 was not in an effort to outshine his brothers but rather to gather information on why everyone was so timid to confront the uncircumcised Philistine Goliath. Because his brothers knew they were incapable of defeating Goliath, they became even more irate towards David for coming down to the battle and asking questions, acting as if he could win against a 9ft giant. David did not once allow his brothers' ignorance to hinder his pursuit in defeating Goliath. David knew who he was, and he stood firm in that knowledge.

What has the Lord called you to conquer? Have you conquered it yet? If not, who are you allowing to hinder you? A small mind can only produce small thoughts because of its capacity. David's brothers would have worked hard over the years to cultivate a physique that would qualify them for battle, but this time the victory was contingent upon a backative that surpassed the physical man and the physical realm. His brothers did not understand this, but David did, and so he was persistent about getting King Saul's approval to step into the fight and put an end to the attempted mockery against Israel. Even King Saul did not understand David's vision. David had to quickly go over his 'animal-fighting' resume to persuade Saul that his experience in the field coupled with his fear of God were qualifications enough to put an end to Goliath in an instant. Saul tried to convince David that his physical stature already made him a victim, but David was steadfast in his belief and pushed further, removing every piece of armored weight Saul tried to clothe him in. It is hard enough when someone does not understand the greatness on the inside of you, but it is even more difficult to try and convince someone of that greatness. Saul soon realized that his efforts to try and 'protect' David remained futile, so he decided to send him out in the battle to prove himself.

I believe those on the outskirts looking in would have already declared doom and gloom for Israel because of David's stature. They could only see the size of his natural body but not the size of his faith, courage and trust in God. They could not see the spiritual giant that was embodied in David's physical stature. The same is true for some of us today. We struggle to fit in and be accepted by those around us, not understanding that small minds can only produce thoughts that are of the same magnitude.

People may have written you off because they only saw a small stature, a small bank account, a small car, a small business but what they failed to see was the big God behind the seemingly small things. It is important to understand that not everyone who has sight, has vision. Sight and vision are different things. Many people have sight but lack vision. They have eyes but are spiritually blind. They cannot envision victory for themselves so it is extremely hard for them to visualize victory for others. When we expect others to see what we see and they don't, it can cause us to feel sad and discouraged. However, we need to allow God to carefully align us with those who possess the capacity to think big—beyond the natural realm. They are the ones who can relate to the seemingly impossible dream or goal, because the Lord would have had them on a similar journey.

Because of David's undaunting pursuit, the 9ft giant was defeated in the most unprecedented way and the rest was history. This story also shows us that they won't believe until it's done.

I'll now share a very personal experience with you. I remember hearing the Lord speak to me concerning a business that He was going to birth through me. I knew it was God because at the time, all I had was a strong passion for the culinary and pastry arts but not as much skill to own an actual business in that industry. I knew it would take much stretching from me to see this vision become a reality and so, I relied on the Holy Spirit to write my entire business plan. Every skill I learned after this encounter was by virtue of the Holy Spirit. It was also at that time that the Lord told me to write and publish my first book, '*The Unveiling.*'

I also remember sharing my grand business idea with a family member who I thought understood the greatness on my life. After sharing my idea, it was met with comparison to others who were in a similar industry. Though I was taken aback by the response I did not allow it to deter me; it was like gas in my tank that propelled me to push further. I don't think the family member had evil intentions towards me, but of course it struck a chord especially when I ran the same idea by another person unrelated to me and they immediately became ecstatic about it. It was eye-opening to have received a more encouraging response from a stranger. The conviction I had about this business venture was stronger than the doubts from my environment. I was challenged to raise my self-confidence to a level that would automatically attract others to do the same. This was what David did; he realized he could not fully convince Saul that He could defeat Goliath so he decided to demonstrate it by defeating him before their very eyes.

> ***"Then Jesus told them, A prophet is honored everywhere except in his own hometown and among his relatives and his own family." (Mark 6:4, NLT)***

On this path of greatness, may we never become discouraged by others' opinion of our ability to succeed. Instead, may we use their disbelief towards you as fuel to propel you forward. When God gives you a vision, many people will not understand it, not even family members. Many times, we look for support from our families because we believe that if anyone should know us better than anyone else, it should be our family members. The sad truth is that this is not always so. Regardless of who supports us or not, God is depending on us to answer the call of greatness.

CHAPTER 3:

STEWARDING PURPOSE

"And it came to pass, that after three days they found him in the temple, sitting in the midst of the doctors, both hearing them, and asking them questions. And all that heard him were astonished at his understanding and answers." (Luke 2: 46, KJV).

Stewarding purpose is an intentional act. To steward your gifts and abilities means you are actively putting measures in place to improve and develop in those areas. The above mentioned verse speaks about Jesus, who at the age of twelve (12) years, went out to the temple. He was so fascinated by the powerful gifts and abilities He possessed that He would spend days in the temple sharing knowledge and seeking to harness His skills. The verse continued by saying that all who heard Jesus speak thought that He was wise and that His knowledge was advanced for his age. This was the result of submerging Himself in the things of God. It is clear that Jesus understood the concept of being a steward. From the beginning, He knew what His mandate was, and that it was not about Him. Stewardship is an act of managing something that belongs to someone else. As a steward, His responsibility was clear—He was commissioned to carefully manage that which was entrusted to Him. Sneaking away to go to the temple was one of the ways 12-year-old Jesus saw it fit to learn and grow in His calling. One of the most important aspects of stewardship is not so much the doing or performing, but it is the learning, growing and developing. Our generation is filled with people who are so eager to 'do', that they skip the preparation step. Yes, you may be anointed to become the greatest C.E.O of all time but have you given yourself to training, guidance, mentorship? Have you sought the face of the Lord for direction on how to accomplish this? What have you done to align yourself with the mandate? We should not make ourselves so occupied to the point where the Lord is not able to speak to us.

In the process of stewarding purpose, it is important to know that training is crucial. The Holy Spirit can train us in the areas of our giftings when we make time for Him. Additionally, the Holy Spirit may lead us to seek training from like-minded people so as to help us improve, sharpen and harness our giftings. If we fail to submit ourselves to teaching and training, we would have truly failed ourselves in the area of stewarding purpose. No human has the capacity to possess all knowledge. In other words, no one person knows everything. No matter how good we think we are, there is always room for improvement, therefore, we should always be open and willing to learn. It is incumbent on us to do the best with what the Lord has given us, and a part of that is to multiply what we have so that we can produce more.

Matthew 25 verses 14 - 30, speaks of the parable of the talents, where the servant who received the one talent, buried it to 'preserve it' because he thought it was fragile and may get lost. However, this was a wrong approach. His action represented a fear of success, and as such it made him immobile towards his purpose. Preserving greatness is in no way equivalent to a fear of success, immobility or stagnation. The act of burying a treasure so as to 'preserve it' knowing that he was called to be a steward over it, shows that he either did not understand the value of the treasure, did not truly appreciate the treasure, or he was just lazy. May this kind of attitude never be named among us. May we not 'lay to rest' that which God has endowed upon us.

I pray you will never allow your mind to talk you out of stewarding the one talent that has great potential to produce more than you could imagine if you put it to good use.

In the same parable, the other servant was given two talents, and he went and produced two more thereby increasing it. This servant could very well view his two talents as insufficient in comparison to the servant who received five, but he didn't. Instead, he was excited to see what the value of his talents were and the returns they would generate. Likewise, the servant who received the five talents went and put them to work so it could be multiplied. There is just something beautiful about having confidence in what you carry. What you carry is gold, since it is the Lord who has blessed you with it. Repeat this seven times until it resonates in your spirit:

"What I Carry is Gold."

"What I Carry is Gold."

"What I Carry is Gold."

"What I Carry is Gold."

"What I Carry is Gold."

"What I Carry is Gold."

"What I Carry is Gold."

What you carry is Gold not because I asked you to repeat it, but because it is the Creator of the Universe who has given it to you. He has blessed you with this gift for you to produce more and bring glory to His name.

> ***"When Elkanah next took his family on their annual trip to Shiloh to worship God, offering sacrifices and keeping his vow, Hannah didn't go. She told her husband, "After the child is weaned, I'll bring him myself and present him before God—and that's where he'll stay, for good." (1 Samuel 1: 21-22, MSG).***

Hannah prayed for a child—a purpose child. She knew that her child would not be like everyone else. Hannah knew that this child would be great and so she had to fulfill her promise to God by taking the child to the temple to hand him over to Eli after the child's birth.

> ***"They first butchered the bull, then brought the child to Eli. Hannah said, "Excuse me, sir. Would you believe that I'm the very woman who was standing***

before you at this very spot, praying to God? I prayed for this child, and God gave me what I asked for. And now I have dedicated him to God. He's dedicated to God for life." Then and there, they worshiped God." (1 Samuel 1:25-28, MSG)

Could Hannah not have raised her child herself in a godly environment? Of course she could, but Hannah made a covenant with the Lord, and she knew it was important to fulfill this promise. Her son Samuel, was anointed to be a prophet to Israel. He was chosen for this mandate even before he was conceived and so his mother saw it fit to leave him in the hands of Eli who would help to harness his spiritual gift and abilities. Samuel did not allow pride to seep in as he grew older. Instead, he sat under the ministry and training of Eli until it was time for his announcement. As a result, Samuel was able to develop the character of a true prophet—one marked by humility, integrity, and accuracy as a mouth-piece of God. His God-given mandate coupled with his willingness to stay in the place of training and mentorship, gave him favor with God and man, and Samuel grew fearless in delivering the word of God to His people. In the words of Apostle James Kawalya, *"It is a gift that opens a nation but it's your character that keeps you there, and it is the fruit that will let you possess the land."* Whatever purpose drives your life should motivate you to seek higher learning and training from godly, reputable people.

> ***"And Joshua the son of Nun was full of wisdom; for Moses had laid his hands upon him: and the children of Israel hearkened unto him: and did as the Lord***

commanded Moses." (Deuteronomy 34:9, KJV)

Joshua was first introduced in scripture in Exodus 17 when he worked alongside Moses, obeying his command to prepare for battle against the Amalekites.

"And Moses said unto Joshua, Choose us out men, and go out, fight with Amalek: tomorrow I will stand on the top of the hill with the rod of God in mine hand. So Joshua did as Moses had said to him, and fought with Amalek: and Moses, Aaron, and Hur went up to the top of the hill." (Exodus 17:9-10 KJV)

Joshua understood that though he was called to be a great leader, he needed actual training. Joshua understood the importance of 'shadowing' Moses, because he knew that if he was going to operate in an office similar to that of Moses then it would be beneficial for him to get hands-on training. As a result, he humbled himself to follow the commands of Moses so that he could learn. Joshua embodied a very important quality called humility. Humility plays an integral role in stewarding purpose. Many of us know what we are called to do but we refuse to submit ourselves to serving our current leaders due to pride. Pride can keep the door of elevation closed. Those who will be great leaders must first be great servants and humility is the key to achieve this. If you find it hard to submit under someone's ministry because you think you know more than they do, you should ask yourself this question, “Why is he or she the leader if I know more than they know?” After asking yourself this question, I hope your answer will be similar to that of, “There is something that they know that I don't know yet but need to know." In fact, leadership is not only about knowledge. Great leaders possess other qualities such as courage, integrity, emotional intelligence and interpersonal skills. While some of these qualities can be taught, one must have an innate people-oriented personality that is motivated by the desire to see people succeed. So though you may be more knowledgeable, it is imperative that you submit to your leader to glean the most you can. Many people want the title and the accolades but do not understand the level of tenacity needed to maintain the role of a leader. So while we wait on our call to leadership, let us steward well and serve with excellence.

The Lord's desire is for us to achieve mastery in the area of our giftings. Sometimes the Lord will cause us to go through a kind of preparation that does not seem to be related to our future position. However, it is necessary that we master every level of preparation because with God nothing is wasted. Though we see in the natural, God sees the benefit of every perceived 'insignificant' step. Not every king will be trained in a palace, and not every warrior will be trained with swords and spears. David was anointed to be king at a young age but he did not take on kingly duties immediately after ordination. He had to go through years of preparation in the field, although he would eventually be seated in the palace. David had to contend with lions and bears on a daily basis—the training that the Lord saw fit to prepare David for the throne. Like David, you may have to go through a training that seems contrary to your calling but is necessary to build your character. This means that we should not despise our beginnings, no matter how small and insignificant they may seem (Zechariah 4:10).

Immediately after Moses died, the Lord spoke to Joshua. It was now time for him to continue what Moses had started. This wasn't a time for Joshua to prepare, it was a time for him to take action. Had Joshua not committed himself to the training Moses provided when he was alive, he would not have been equipped to be his successor. Moses' wisdom, skills and abilities, and all the ways in which the Lord had used him, were now required for Joshua to carry the mantle that was previously carried by his predecessor.

If we are to steward purpose well, we must understand the importance of times and seasons (Eccl 3:1). Therefore, it is imperative to seize every opportunity and avoid procrastination at all costs. We must manage our resources well and not entertain people who will try to kill or stifle our purpose.

As we take hold of the opportune times and seasons, we will be better able to maximize that which the Lord has given to us. We will be able to discern and detect the move of God because we will be on the same wavelength as Him. We will be where God is and not where God was. Though God exists outside of time, He will speak to us in a specific time and give us instructions on the way forward. It is necessary for us to prepare for whatever He has instructed us to do. Failing to prepare will cause us to be left behind when the season comes for us to manifest the glory of God. This is why we cannot afford to waste time. We cannot afford to waste time trying to seek approval from people who don't even have a relationship with God. We cannot afford to waste time doing nothing while waiting for God to come and do it for us. We cannot afford to waste time with the wrong crowd trying to fit in. We cannot afford to waste time pursuing a purpose that is similar to that of our friend's because we think that what God called us to do is not cool enough. We cannot afford to waste time complaining that we lack resources to fulfill the purpose. From now on, we will make every effort to be in sync with the Spirit of God. We will no longer be staggering outside of the will of God wondering when it will be our time to fulfill purpose, but we will make every second count by spending time in His presence. We will carefully align ourselves with His purpose for our lives and we will liaise with godly people of similar calling to help us harness the gifts within and bring glory to God. Be committed to using the 'little' that the Lord has given to you. Manage it well so that it can be increased and your impact on the earth can be far-reaching.

CHAPTER 4:

THE ISOLATION

“SHH, NOT YET...”

Imagine receiving a revelation about yourself that you were totally oblivious to. Most if not all of us would be eager to share this great news with others we love and trust. As human beings, we have the tendency to make announcements when we are excited. However, there is a time and place for announcements. Sometimes the Lord wants us to keep quiet even in the midst of our good news, because what He plans to do has not yet been done or what He is doing is not yet completed. Additionally, sometimes God wants to be the announcer so He can get the glory for Himself.

Preserving greatness and stewarding purpose comes with a period called 'Isolation'. Isolation is that stage in the process of greatness where the Lord calls us away from the crowd to prune us and train us for the next level. Does isolation feel good? Absolutely not. During isolation, people may assume you have been rejected or reaping the consequences of your sins but this is not always the case. There is a difference between isolation influenced by the consequences of one's sins and God-induced isolation which is to allow you to become whole and mature–lacking nothing (James 1:4).

Isolation can be understood from the analogy of a farmer who plants his seed into the ground. When a farmer decides to sow a seed, the seed has to be buried in the dark earth where the seed becomes isolated for a period of time. Onlookers may have given the seed a particular time to protrude through the ground and become a plant. They may also think that if the seed does not spring up at that time, it may be no good and will never grow to produce fruit. Despite what the onlookers believe, the farmer has to remain confident that the seed will produce. He is not troubled by the opinions of others because he knows that every fruit tree has a specific germination period and he also knows the quality of the seed he has placed inside the earth. In addition, he has a different perspective on the 'death' of the seed, in that death is necessary for new life to spring from it.

I use this analogy of the seed to describe isolation in a positive light. Isolation, though viewed as an endless torture, has the ability to reap worthwhile rewards. Even Jesus isolated Himself to spend time in prayer. This underscores the power of isolation.

> ***"Before daybreak the next morning, Jesus got up and went out to an isolated place to pray." (Mark 1:35, NLT)***

Though isolation does not feel good, it is necessary for preserving greatness. It is important to know that when a seed is in a period of isolation, the seed lacks nothing. All it needs for growth is provided in the soil. Similarly, a believer must know that all he or she needs is already provided in their place of isolation. Although it is important for us to interact with people on a day to day basis, isolation is more important because limiting daily interactions with people to spend more time in the presence of God is a priority. Isolation is a necessary step to become who God has called you to become.

What God is calling you to be cannot be attained by always giving others most of your time and leaving the leftovers for God. God wants all of your attention. It was Apostle Joshua Selman who said that, *"The Price For All of God is All of You."*

> ***"Then Jesus was led by the Spirit into the wilderness to be tempted there by the devil. For***

forty days and forty nights he fasted and became very hungry". (Matt 4:1-2, NLT)

Jesus knew what it felt like to be isolated. Before God lifts a man He will isolate them to train them. Jesus was being trained for His lifting. Isolation also works in conjunction with consecration. Joshua told the people to consecrate themselves for the Lord is about to do a great work among them.

"Joshua told the people, "Consecrate yourselves, for tomorrow the LORD will do amazing things among you." (Joshua 3:5, NIV)

God does not isolate us to make us feel lonely, abandoned or unsafe. He isolates us for His good will. Isolation is necessary for death, growth and maturity. Additionally, when the Lord calls us out of a crowd, it is for a reason. Not everyone around us can go with us to where the Lord is taking us.

> ***"And as they were going down to the end of the city, Samuel said to Saul, Bid the servant pass lon before us (and he passed on,) but stand thou still a while, that I may shew thee the word of God." (1 Samuel 9:27, KJV)***

In the above-mentioned verse, Samuel could have very well made the announcement of Saul 'becoming king' in the presence of Saul's servant but that was not the approach the Lord wanted him to take. Instead, Samuel instructed the servant to go ahead of them so he could speak to Saul in private. Not everything the Lord reveals to you should be shared with those around you in the moment, not because you are greater or lesser than they are, but because the Lord knows all things and has a set time for them to take place. While the Lord is working on and in you, revealing Himself to you through miraculous encounters, stay the course in silence, unannounced until He releases you to the public.

> ***"And they lifted up their voice and wept again: and Orpah kissed her mother in law; but Ruth clave unto her." (Ruth 1:14, KJV)***

Ruth 1:14 summarizes the character of Ruth in a nutshell. Ruth was one of those 'ride or die' individuals. She was determined to stick with her mother-in-law even though her husband had died. Ruth knew the true meaning of loyalty. Her loyalty did not end when her husband's life ended. Though Naomi wanted the best for Ruth, Ruth decided that she would take care of her mother-in-law and never leave her side. It was through her determination to stay with her mother- in -law that led her to Boaz.

Now if we recall the story correctly, we will see that Ruth went through her own season of isolation. Not only did she lose her husband, her brothers-in-law and father-in-law but she lost her source of income, considering she was now in a new town, Bethlehem. As a result of this, Ruth went out into the fields to glean barley on a daily basis so that she and her mother-in-law could have food. It was during her quest to find food that she was noticed by a wealthy man named Boaz. Ruth had no knowledge of Boaz nor was she aware of his wealth prior to this. She only dedicated herself to gleaning in the field, but little did she know that the Lord was preparing her during this time to be the help-meet for Boaz. Ruth endured her season of isolation and was rewarded for it.

"The LORD had said to Abram, Go from your country, your people and your father's household to the land I will show you." (Gen 12:1, NIV).

Abraham went through his season of isolation when the Lord instructed him to get out of his country to go to a foreign place. Instead of questioning the instructions of the Lord, Abraham willingly obeyed. He left his country where everyone knew him, to go to a place he had no knowledge of.

When God wants to elevate you, he will take you through a season of isolation to train you so you can develop the right character and discipline. The Lord wanted to enlarge Abraham's territory and make him the father of many nations, but it was necessary for him to do his part in order to obtain the promise. In the process, Abraham encountered a lot of setbacks, but despite the setbacks, Abraham endured. Since God had already pronounced generational blessings on Abraham, it was impossible for Abraham to be cursed. Had Abraham not obeyed the instructions of God, he would not have been able to reap the blessings that came with the promise. While he may have anticipated the blessings that followed his obedience, he may not have anticipated the isolation that came with the blessings. Many of us today want to be blessed but not many of us want to be built. It is through the process of isolation that qualities such as patience, faith, character and integrity are built.

> ***"...or ministry, let us wait on our ministering: or he that teacheth, on teaching; or he that exhorteth, on exhortation: he that giveth, let him do it with simplicity; he that ruleth, with***

diligence; he that sheweth mercy, with cheerfulness. Romans 12: 7-8, KJV).

In Romans 12:7-8, Paul encouraged the believers to wait on their ministry and Isaiah 40:31 tells us the benefits of waiting upon God. There is great reward in waiting on God; staying in His presence praying, worshiping, reading the Word. Oftentimes we are of the belief that we should start ministering the moment a man or woman of God lays hands on us, but this is not so. Prophesying and the laying on of hands are done to bring knowledge, edification and also preparation for ministry. This should propel us to prepare ourselves in such a way that when it's time to actually start our ministry we would have been trained and ready to go. In the words of Apostle Grace Lubega, *"If you have questions about what you were called to be, wait on God; if you want to transition from the called to the chosen, wait on God; if you want to know the key milestones of your life and ministry, wait on God."*

If you are currently going through a season of isolation, be encouraged that it is for your good. After this season of isolation, rest assured that you will come out victorious. This season is not to kill you but to build you. Though you may cry, or dread the process, it is necessary for your development. Think about how risky it would be for an untrained soldier to enter the battlefield. We can even think about how frustrating it would be for someone who enters a new school or new job without proper orientation, job description or any material to tell them what they are to do. This is not only risky, but it sets that person up for failure. When you do not know what to do, it sets you up to make mistakes and God does not want that for you. He knows the price of the calling. He knows that an unprepared believer is open to dangerous attacks from the enemy. God wants to equip us in such a way that when we go out on the battlefield of our ministry, we are not ignorant of the enemy's devices.

Saul vs David

If we look at the lives of Saul and David individually before they became kings, we will notice that David had been on training ground for this position all his life. Though it was God's intention for Saul to be the kind of king that would prove to Israel that God was and will always be their king, it also shows us that Saul did not get much preparation to be the king that Israel needed. There is something special about going through the season of preparation. While going through the season of preparation, many people may be prone to walk away from it because it is always an opportune time for the enemy to whisper convincing lies to them. You may currently be going through this process, and you are wondering when it will be over.

To encourage you, I'd like to use the analogy of fruit trees and their germination period through to the time of bearing. Research shows that for mango trees, their germination period ranges between 2-4 weeks but may take up to 5 years to bear fruit. For apple trees, the germination period also ranges between 2-4 weeks but can take up to 7 years to bear a single fruit. Do you see the major time difference? While we are all gifted and possess great talents, our germination and fruit-bearing periods will have specific times depending on what we carry. Like the apple tree, a very common fruit that many have grown to love, many of you are in your process of germination right now, this is why you are being isolated. It is so that you will reach spiritual maturation. In addition, just as waiting on a fruit for up to 5 years requires patience, so too you will have to exercise patience until the seed of purpose starts bearing fruit.

Growing up, I'd often see failed relationships and marriages to the point of getting scared of marriage even for myself. Over the years, I have observed that people were more engrossed in the preparation of the wedding ceremony but not necessarily the actual "work" - the marriage, that comes thereafter. In the words of Benjamin Franklin, "*If we fail to prepare,*" we automatically "*prepare to fail.*" What God called us to do cannot be accomplished without submitting ourselves to proper training. Though the process of isolation may feel as if it is taking forever, rest assured that you will emerge victorious in the end. So, if the Lord has not announced you yet, "Shh, it's not time yet. Endure!"

CHAPTER 5:

DEATH & HUMILITY

Death is one of the most crucial parts of life. For anything to be great, it first has to die. For anyone to live a meaningful life that pleases God, he or she must first be willing to die— to self, the flesh and sin. One of the benefits of death is that the life that is resurrected from it, is now one lived for the cause of Christ. It is a life that is not easily offended and now has the capacity to contain all of God and not just a part of Him. For some Christians, death takes place during the process of isolation. However, it can take place before, during or after. The Lord is looking for people who are willing to die in order to live for Him. An individual who is too alive to self cannot truly please Christ. If we are too alive, we will walk in our own ways and not the ways of Christ. Our flesh will lead us to follow a path that we 'think' will lead us to our greatness—an idea we were socialized to believe.

Through socialization we gain knowledge on how to operate in social settings, we learn different social roles, and we become more culturally aware. While this information is important, the person who will fully submit to God must understand that God operates outside of human logic. He operates with vessels that are willing to die to flesh and its desires. But there is a battle, because the demon of our flesh constantly wages war against our spirit and tries to manipulate it into thinking that if something doesn't make 'the flesh' feel good then it's not worth keeping. The truth is that there is nowhere in scripture where the Bible promotes the work of flesh. In fact, it admonishes us that the fruit of the flesh leads to eternal damnation and death.

Now this kind of death is different from the one previously mentioned, in that dying to flesh is different from dying due to the flesh. The death that Christ requires is one that kills the carnal and amplifies the spiritual. It is a death that terminates sin and transgression in our mortal bodies, and produces humility.

> ***"The greatest among you will be your servant. For those who exalt themselves will be humbled, and those who humble themselves will be exalted." (Matthew 23:11-12, KJV).***

Not only does this verse show us that humility is tied to greatness but it also shows the posture and disposition of those who are great. Those who are great have learned to submit themselves to their superiors in humility. They don't mind serving others, because it is through serving they expand their scope of knowledge and gain hands-on experience. Those who are great understand that serving does not make them less of a great person. Rather, it sets them up for promotion. Since it is God who exalts and abases, He is the one who has the power to promote and demote, and He will promote them in due time.

> ***"For promotion cometh neither from the east, nor from the west, nor from the south. But God is the judge; he putteth down one, and setteth up another." (Psalm 75:6-7, KJV)***

Not many of us desire the role of a servant because it is often seen as someone with less privileges than the average human being. Servants are most times viewed as inferior and dealt with in a condescending manner and treated unequally. Contrary to this world's view, the Bible encourages us to have a servant's heart; one that is willing to love and serve others at all times.

"But Jesus called them together and said, "You know that the rulers in this world lord it over their people, and officials flaunt their authority over those under them. But among you it will be different. Whoever wants to be a leader among you must be your servant, and whoever wants to be first among you must become your slave. For even the Son of Man came not to be served but to serve others and to give his life as a ransom for many." (Matt 20:25-28, NLT)

In the text above, Jesus outlined the way in which service should be done. He explained to His disciples that their view of power and authority should not be the same as the world sees it. Those in the world who exert superiority over a group of people may at times abuse their power to gain respect. Jesus told the disciples that there should be a different approach for those who desire to be leaders in the body of Christ. This approach should convey true humility in that anyone who desires to lead, must first be trained as a servant. Perhaps this approach will allow prospective leaders to show more compassion towards those who serve them. Whatever the reason for his instructions, Jesus himself was an example to show the disciples that He came not to be served but to serve. True servants will serve even when others do not treat them well. Jesus was oftentimes opposed, accused and threatened by the Pharisees. There were instances where they would ask him questions in a particular way for him to contradict Himself, but Jesus was wiser than their minds could perceive. Despite their many attempts to destroy Jesus's life and ministry, Jesus remained steadfast in serving.

Due to the negative connotation attached to the word 'servant,' not many people desire to be servants. However, servanthood is one of the greatest roles one could have. This is the posture that the Lord expects us to have. He knows that in order to lead, we first have to develop character through servanthood, which is characterized by humility, an important key to greatness.

> ***"Let this mind be in you, which was also in Christ Jesus: Who, being in the form of God, thought it not robbery to be equal with God: But made himself of no reputation, and took upon him the form of a servant, and was made in the likeness of men: And being found in fashion as a man, he***

humbled himself, and became obedient unto death, even the death of the cross. Wherefore God also hath highly exalted him, and given him a name which is above every name:" (Philippians 2:5-9, KJV).

In verse 7 of the above-mentioned verse, Jesus took on the attitude of a servant. Jesus is the perfect representation of the word humility because He demonstrated the true meaning of dying to self. One cannot truly take on the character of humility without dying first—dying to our unholy desires, dying to our toxic habits that keep us in unhealthy cycles and dying to our feelings and preferences in an attempt to please others.

Humility is the ladder to GREATNESS. Philippians 2: 5-9 suggests that humility is connected to elevation, exaltation, promotion, increase, and commendation. This means that humility cannot co-exist with pride. According to Luke 14:11, pride de-elevates, abases, demotes, decreases, causes embarrassment. It simply does the opposite of what being humble attracts. As people who were created to be GREAT, we must understand that after the season of isolation, humility is now required for us to walk in power and manifest the glory of God in the earth.

God hates pride! According to Proverbs 6:16-19, the Bible lists seven things that the Lord hates and of the seven things, haughty eyes (which is pride), was mentioned as the very first one. The word haughty is synonymous with proud, high-minded and arrogant. God is omniscient; He knows the things that have the ability to impact us in a negative way. He also knows how to properly train us in order for us to not fall prey to these things. Pride is so dangerous that it got Lucifer kicked out of heaven. God wants to save us from the consequence that comes with being proud. This is why we must always embody humility, even when the Lord announces us, and we are finally walking through the doors that were once closed on us.

For some people, it may not require much effort for them to be humble when they don't have all that they need, but it may take a lot of discipline for them to remain humble when God has blessed them with all the things that they need. Demonstrating humility during a time of plenty is a true test of character. I remember a time the Lord spoke to me during the pandemic and said, "Favor will give you access to the blessings, but humility is what will allow you to maintain the blessings." I then fell into a trance and the Lord showed me practically what that meant. What I saw was a ladder going all the way up to the top of a house and the feet of an individual climbing upwards. Instead of having actual steps, the ladder had the word 'humility' where the steps should be. The Lord showed me that humility is what keeps an individual in an elevated position, and the moment they allow pride to replace humility, the steps immediately disappeared, and that individual becomes prone to falling all the way back to the ground. This shows that pride and humility cannot coexist.

Humility is a key ingredient in the process of greatness. Both Saul and David were kings at different stages of their lives, but it was clear that David displayed more humility than Saul. There are a few scriptures that highlight David's heart posture. For example, 1 Samuel 30:1- 8 (MSG) showed David's humility and obedience in the midst of turmoil.

"Three days later, David and his men arrived back in Ziklag. Amalekites had raided the Negev and Ziklag. They tore Ziklag to pieces and then burned it down. They captured all the women, young and old. They didn't kill anyone, but drove them like a herd of cattle. By the time David and his men entered the village, it had been burned to the ground, and their wives, sons, and daughters all taken prisoner.

David and his men burst out in loud wails—wept and wept until they were exhausted with weeping. David's two wives, Ahinoam of Jezreel and Abigail widow of Nabal of Carmel, had been taken prisoner along with the rest. And suddenly David

was in even worse trouble. There was talk among the men, bitter over the loss of their families, of stoning him.

David strengthened himself with trust in his God. He ordered Abiathar the priest, son of Ahimelech, "Bring me the Ephod so I can consult God." Abiathar brought it to David.

Then David prayed to God, "Shall I go after these raiders? Can I catch them?" (1 Samuel 30:1- 8, MSG).

Instead of making an impulsive decision to chase after the Amalekites, David chose to consult with God first. This was a notable act because not only had they taken David's wives and possessions but also the possessions of his men. As a result, his men considered stoning him; blaming him for what had happened. But in the midst of this chaotic situation, David yielded his will to that of God instead of acting out of his emotions. No wonder the bible refers to him as a man after God's own heart. David's acts of humility and obedience were very evident. As a result, the Lord caused him to recover all he and his men had lost.

Another notable bible character who displayed humility was Solomon. Solomon displayed humility when he got the opportunity to request anything from God. Instead of asking God for something that would satisfy his immediate desires, he asked God for wisdom to know how to rule over the people. Perhaps Solomon had an experience with injustice, or probably he was just a selfless king. Whichever it was, Solomon did well in making his request for wisdom. This shows that he was looking at the bigger picture. Solomon understood the vast difference between leading a family versus leading a whole nation. Though wisdom is essential for the leading of one's family, it takes another dimension of wisdom to lead a whole nation. Because he asked for wisdom instead of material gain, the Lord gave him more than he asked for. This shows us that the Lord rewards unselfish actions. Selflessness is an attribute of humility. To produce true humility, an individual must first die to himself, and secondly, be willing to serve others with genuine intentions. If we look closely at Solomon's posture in this case, it was not self-seeking but more of seeking the welfare of others.

While humility is not self-seeking, this does not mean that it totally ignores the needs of oneself. We live in a world where people tend to display false humility in an effort to prove to others that they are humble. The truth is that a person who is truly humble does not need to prove it to others. Contrary to the beliefs of others, humility takes into consideration selfcare. In order to serve others, we need to first take care of ourselves. Our mental, emotional and physical health are of utmost importance when thinking of serving others. This is because without being mentally, emotionally and physically well, we are automatically disqualified from being in a position to serve others, even if we are financially well. Without good mental, emotional and physical health, most if not all our thought patterns and decisions will be affected, thereby affecting our quality of service.

As you begin to shed the flesh and produce humility, allow the word of God to guide you. Do not take on the world's idea of humility as it is not genuine and will not produce godly results. The world's view of humility seeks to serve only those who are nice to you but morphs into a whole different being when someone is mean to you. In contrast, the word of God admonishes us to love our neighbor as ourselves (Mark 12:31), bless those who curse us (Luke 6:28), and forgive others even as our Father in heaven has forgiven us (Matt 6:9).

CHAPTER 6:

RISE TO THE OCCASION

"And so, after he had patiently endured, he obtained the promise." (Hebrews 6:15, KJV)

After a turbulently long period of isolation characterized by screeching silence and overwhelming solitude where death takes place and humility is produced, God will announce you! This is when you will rise to the occasion and walk in your God-given purpose—the same purpose you have been stewarding over the years and being trained to walk into. In the above mentioned verse, Abraham obtained the promise due to his patient endurance. This shows us that God will not allow us to go through death in vain. Even the resurrection story shows us that in order to rise, you first have to die. That is what this chapter is about—rising with intent, rising from impurity, rising from self to walk in our divine destiny. As we prepare to rise to the occasion and embrace the greatness on our lives, we must identify the level to which we were called so that we do not rise to a higher level of subordination.

When we rise to the occasion, we are rising with wisdom. This wisdom comes from understanding the price we have paid and the price we continue to pay in order to walk in this greatness. If we never had to fight for it, endure pain for it, lose sleep for it, then we will never know the value of it when we obtain it. We develop a sense of appreciation when we see the result of our blood, sweat and tears—the reward of our hard work. For us to experience the feeling of accomplishment that comes from enduring to obtain the promise, we must stay faithful throughout our isolation period. Those who forfeit their season of isolation are often premature and self-proclaimed. However, those who patiently endure will rise with maturity and humility.

As mentioned in a previous chapter, every seed that becomes a fruit first had to go through isolation and death. When it rises and bursts through the Earth, we know that it is time for it to grow intentionally. Similar to a seed, humans who go through isolation will find that some shedding has taken place. If we remain diligent in submitting ourselves to the hard parts of our process, in due time we will be empowered to rise to a higher dimension of greatness.

Rising to the occasion is for those who would have endured the periods of isolation and embraced the lessons that came with it. Many have tried to rise to the occasion without being properly developed and have fallen as a result. We cannot bypass death and humility and all the lessons they come with and go straight to rising to the occasion. It simply does not work like that. However, when you have fully endured the preparation process, you will be ushered into your rising. The ground would have already been broken for you. God would have already gone ahead of you to make your crooked places straight.

The idea of rising is desirable to the natural human. After all, no one wants to endure pain for too long, no one wants to be hidden or forgotten about for too long. So the word 'rising' is quite desirable to mere men because it connotes a place of elevation free from pain, abandonment and concealment. The mere human would not mind getting rewarded without having to do the actual work. Let's be honest, the actual work is not fun. The actual work takes a lot of 'work' but like a fruit tree we too have our processing time that is required to make us whole, mature, lacking nothing. This is why we should never dread our process of becoming. There are two facts that we are faced with in this process—what we know and what we do not know. What we know is that we will be fully equipped on the other side of our process but the thought of not knowing what day, month or year it will end can trigger frustration and/or the forfeiting of the process.

The issue is further exacerbated when onlookers misunderstand our season of isolation and criticize our process; passing it off as a sin committed or a curse. We should never let this affect our process. People will always find something to talk about but one thing is for certain, no one person will ever talk about the same situation forever. Even Jesus Himself was criticized, but instead of it being a hindrance to His ministry, it was confirmation that He was doing the will of His Father.

In almost all instances there will be naysayers; those onlookers who do not even possess the idea of a vision for themselves but feel entitled to be dictator over the lives of others. Those who are called to be great must not allow the external effects of negativity to get on the inside of them. May you protect the greatness on the inside of you at all cost.

Nehemiah's Undaunting Pursuit to Rebuild

In the book of Nehemiah 4 verses 6 to 15, Nehemiah embodies a true definition rising to the occasion. Nehemiah's position as cupbearer to Artaxerxes had strategically placed him in a role of favor and great honor. As a cupbearer, Nehemiah was close to the king. He was the one responsible for pouring the king's wine and other beverages. This was a good place to meet people from all walks of life and hear of the happenings around him. After hearing of the great affliction faced by the Jews, the destruction of walls of Jerusalem and the burning of its gates, Nehemiah became very burdened in his heart and wept for days. Nehemiah soon resorted to fasting and prayer seeking God for his intervention.

During his prayer, Nehemiah repented on behalf of his father and forefathers. This was a strategic prayer because Nehemiah knew that there were consequences for those who sinned, so after acknowledging their transgression, he cried out to God for mercy. Nehemiah wanted to rebuild the walls. He had gotten heaven's approval, and the king later granted his request for him to go. He was wise enough to know that this was not going to happen without the possibility of opposition, and so he ensured that he got letters signed and sealed by the king to give him access throughout his journey.

After the work began on the wall, Nehemiah and his workmen began to face opposition from Sanballat and Tobiah. It started with them undermining the work, which then spiraled into conspiracy and rumors. Regardless, Nehemiah remained steadfast in the work of God. The wisdom Nehemiah exuded in all of this work was admirable. He rose to the occasion in spite of his adversaries. He was not fazed by the rumors and schemes of his opposers. The louder his enemies got, the more focused Nehemiah became. He had a vision of rebuilding the walls of Jerusalem and nothing was going to hinder his work.

Nehemiah Shares Similar Qualities To That Of A Healthy Tree.

There are some similarities between the quality of a healthy tree and that of a 'riser'. A healthy tree has a solid foundation, and so does a 'riser.' Nehemiah's foundation was firmly built on God. He had already placed the matter before God and so he stood on faith knowing that God would see him through to complete the work. Another quality is that a healthy tree is hard and its hardness reflects its ability to survive environmental conditions. Similarly, Nehemiah's years as cupbearer had prepared him for the rebuilding of the temple. Though he encountered much resistance from his outer environment, he remained faithful. Nehemiah understood the importance of his purpose and was not concerned about the affairs of his enemies. He worked relentlessly, in humility and fear of God.

As a result, he rose to the occasion and took his place in order to bring justice to the oppressed.

Rising to the occasion means that we possess the power to stand against the critiques, naysayers, and just about anything in the environment that would want to belittle our existence. It is important to note that though many may revolt against us, it is not for us to respond to them in the same manner. Since the previous stage would have helped us to shed the components of flesh, it is imperative that we embody God-honoring dispositions in every interaction.

When Sanballat and Tobiah's initial strategy did not work, they sent letters inviting Nehemiah to come and meet with them, a seemingly friendly gesture but Nehemiah was wise enough to know their craftiness and so he refused. This is important because the enemy will try to use different schemes in attempts to overthrow us if we are ignorant to his devices.

> ***"Lest satan should get an advantage of us: for we are not ignorant of his devices." (2 Cor 2: 11, KJV)***

Paul warns us to not be ignorant to the schemes of the enemy. We should never be sidetracked when rising to fulfill our God-given purposes. This is not a time for us to attend the board meeting of the enemy to sign a peace treaty. It is a time to renew our focus, remain persistent and motivated despite the odds. As you can imagine, rising to the occasion to walk into greatness will not be a place of total euphoria where trouble is absent. Instead, it is a place where our character is put on display and any wrong move could cause others to doubt the authenticity of our process. Rising to the occasion requires you to launch out into the deep to pursue everything others said you could not achieve but not letting that be the sole reason for achieving your goals. At this stage, many of the onlookers are not hoping to see you because they may have already pronounced you dead, deficient, unable or incapable.

However, if you stay focused in your rising, you will prove them wrong. It is important for you to know that people who were called to be great do not fight the enemy on his terrain. Instead, they soar to a higher place where the enemy has no chance of reaching. This is where you walk in total confidence knowing that you have all you need to succeed. Fear is dismissed; you no longer possess the capacity to house it anyway, and what you have been through stands as a resounding testimony that heralds your appearance. Be mindful that not everyone will be happy to see you and that is okay. Because of this, your presence will make a lot of doubters unhappy. Respect them and love them anyway.

On the path of greatness, pause if you must but never stop. Remain focused and determined, but expect to be misunderstood. You're not obligated to schedule a meeting with doubters to explain your drive and motivation. The training, isolation, abandonment and belittlement have produced a resilient version of you who has learned to trust and depend on God. This version of you understands that even when close friends and family walk away, you will be in your best position to prosper. This is not because you do not value the support and contribution from relatives and friends, but you have gained experiential knowledge to understand that if God is all you have, then you have all you need. You will also understand that God is strategic in how he positions destiny-helpers in your life.

Your destiny-helpers are not automatically found in your circle of family or friends. In fact, most times it is those in our close circles who tend to fight against our dreams and purposes the most. Sometimes the Lord will use a total stranger who has spiritual knowledge and can see your vision to help you accomplish it, while those with whom you have lived with all your life remain unaware and unsupportive of your purpose and calling. Rise anyway!

CHAPTER 7:

INTENTIONAL LIVING

"For His divine power has bestowed on us [absolutely] everything necessary for [a dynamic spiritual] life and godliness, through true and personal knowledge of Him who called us by His own glory and excellence." (2 Pet 1:3, AMP)

This scripture epitomizes the essence of living intentionally. Other translations state that all we need for life and godliness has been given to us through the knowledge of the giver-God Himself. For a person to live intentionally he/she must be in sync with the Father. Living intentionally means excuses are no longer accepted and you do not apologize for winning or being celebrated. It means showing up clothed in your God-given purpose to dominate while being careful to attribute your success to the faithfulness of God. It is important to live out your purpose rather than trying to fit in. When you develop and maintain an intimate relationship with the Lord, He will show you who you are. Did you know that not everywhere we fit, we are supposed to be?

I recently saw a LinkedIn post that stated, "not because you fit in means you are in the correct place." Upon observing the post, I saw a picture of some clean ceramic plates lined up between the iron racks of a water drain that was on the side of a road. At first glance, the clean plates looked as if they were in a dish drainer inside a kitchen because of how similar the roadside drain resembles the dish drainer in the picture. However, when the outer parts of the picture were observed, it clearly showed that the clean plates were neatly stacked in a water drain along a roadside. I found this to be quite an interesting post because oftentimes we think that because something lines up in a particular space or location, means that is where it is supposed to be. Like this image, it is possible for an individual to be misaligned in a seemingly 'aligned' position. This is a deceptive tactic used by the enemy to get us out of our God-given, God-ordained places of purpose.

Living intentionally can mean different things to different people, it can encapsulate careful preparation, planning, prayer and acting unapologetically. Those who live intentionally examine their decisions to see the kind of outcomes that they will produce and are motivated to create a path for themselves even if there is no trace of a path. When we live intentional lives, we avoid making excuses and instead become responsible managers of the purpose God has given to us. The value we place on our time may be misunderstood by others, but we know that the God who entrusts us with our purpose is depending on us to make good decisions that will cause it to multiply and produce twenty, fifty, one hundred or even one thousandfold.

Apostle Paul Lived An Intentional Life

Unlike other human beings whose natural response to pain is to withdraw and/or express an unpleasant emotion, Paul welcomes pain as an honor for the sake of Christ. Paul is characterized by his unrelenting, unwavering pursuit to preach the gospel of Christ. As a man of wisdom, he knew that there was a heavenly reward, and so he was motivated to press toward the mark for the prize of the higher calling (Phil 3:14). He endured suffering and persecution with great grace and never looked back after his conversion. Paul understood that there was a price to pay for choosing Christ. God converted Paul's passion for persecuting the church into preaching the gospel. God did not change the intensity of his passion, He only changed the way he used it.

Paul's intentional life was admirable because he understood that life was loaned to him. This is supported by Philippians 1:21 where Paul wrote, ***"For to me to live is Christ, and to die is gain." (Phil 1:21 KJV).*** Paul counted it as an honor to suffer persecution for Christ which reveals to us that he considered his life an instrument totally in the hands of God. Similar to this, Peter wrote that ***"There's no particular virtue in accepting punishment that you well deserve. But if you're treated badly for good behavior and continue in spite of it to be a good servant, that is what counts with God." (1 Peter 2:20, MSG).*** Peter said this in an effort to explain that there is a difference between being persecuted for doing the right thing versus being persecuted for doing the wrong thing. Paul was doing the work of God. He was a straightforward minister of the gospel who was not afraid to call a spade a spade. Though he was stoned, shipwrecked, bitten by a scorpion, beaten on several occasions, none of these hindered Paul from preaching the gospel and doing the work of the Lord. It is obvious that Paul understood the purpose for which he was called. Since he understood his purpose, he could not allow the rejection from others to stop what God had started in him.

Unfortunately, this is where a lot of believers struggle. Noone ever told us that living for Christ was a smooth road without obstacles. In fact, the Bible tells us in many ways that living for God will come with its tests and trials. Luke 14:28

encourages us to count the cost before taking on a task.

"Suppose one of you wants to build a tower. Wont you first sit down and estimate the cost to see if you have enough money to complete it." (Luke 14:28, NIV)

Think about the price you will have to pay to see the work completed in you. Likewise, Matthew 16:24 (KJV) informs us that those who will come to Christ will first have to deny themselves, take up their cross and follow Jesus.

"Then Jesus said unto his disciples, if any man will come after me, let him deny himself, and take up His cross, and follow me." (Matthew 16:28, KJV).

When you live intentionally, you live truthfully. There should not be incongruence in what you believe and how you live. Ideally, the truth that you live must come from the word of God. In John 14:6, Jesus tells us that He is the way, the TRUTH and the life and that no one can go to father except through Him. One of the ways you do so is by walking confidently in what He says about you.

Romans 8:37 reminds us that in all things we are more than conquerors. I have heard many people affirm themselves with this verse by saying, "I am a conqueror through Jesus", but isn't that an understatement about who we really are? Paul did not just say that we are conquerors but that we are ***"...more than conquerors..." (Romans 8:37 KJV).*** When the depth of this truth hits your spirit, it will stir up an awakening, an enlightenment and will encourage you to keep going.

Those who will live intentionally will live victoriously. Now, this victory does not come by chance. As children of God, we do not win by chance, nor by luck, we win because we are properly aligned with the Word of God. When we believe what it says, though we may face difficult seasons, we remain faithful, endure our season, prepare ourselves and rise with the Word of God in our hearts and determination in our eyes. By living intentionally, we live on purpose, and we celebrate our wins in this phase of life without being consumed by pride, all while attributing the credit for our successes to God.

Discipline Strengthens Intentionality

One of the ways in which we live intentionally is to develop a life of discipline. I must admit that discipline is not as easily attained as it sounds, but it is very important to the journey we are on. A life of discipline will help us to minimize excuses, maximize our potential and manifest our prophecies. Many of us are so accustomed to losing that when the opportunities come for us to start winning, we shy away from them.

Excuses are a Deterrent to Success

I remember the first time I received a request to teach at a high school. This was a long-term goal of mine, but it happened so suddenly I started to find all the excuses possible. I was thinking of all the reasons I could not do it because I only had experience as a pre-k-8th grade teacher, but the opportunity came for me to expand my reach and grow, and I saw it as a threat to my abilities. I came up with all sorts of excuses such as how rude teenagers are and the disrespect I would probably endure as a result. I was trying to cancel myself from the goal that I set out to accomplish in the beginning. At that moment, the Lord rebuked me for my erroneous thinking. I did not realize what I was doing until the Lord spoke to me. It then dawned on me that I was stuck on familiar territory of my past experiences. Instead of seeing it as an opportunity, I saw it as a threat and fear tried to creep in. From this experience, I realized something very profound; many of us do not have the fear of failure, what we have is the fear of success. I share this experience to enlighten you that excuses are a deterrent to your progress and your purpose.

If we should examine ourselves, we will identify the real reasons we sometimes shy away from things that will take us to a higher level. The enemy convinces us that we may fail because we have never done it before. But, what if you do not fail? "What if you succeed? What if you win?" If you attempt it and fail on the first try, that is okay because it becomes a learning experience for you. In fact, you didn't lose, you learned something. So, next time the enemy confronts you with the possibility of failure, combat it with, "What if I win?"

After my first day at the high school, I realized I had a total misconception about the experience I would have— this was a carefully constructed lie from the pit of hell. Although some teenagers have unpleasant attitudes, the same is true for adults. We all have unpleasant attitudes that we need to get rid of. As an educator, I have realized that whatever you serve to your students will reflect in their response to you. If you respect and uplift them, they respond in a like manner.

Our Destinies Were Preordained For Us.

I was born to be an educator. Today, I can confidently say that I have the gift of teaching, but I did not know this until the end of my Psychology degree when the Lord revealed it to me. Unknown to me was that my years of serving in VBS (Vacation Bible School) and Sunday School were my training ground. All I needed was already given to me, but the enemy wanted me to talk myself out of the very thing God had anointed me to do. My destiny was preordained for me and so is yours. Do not fall prey to the enemy's tactic of making excuses. The only place it has a record of taking people is to a place of stagnancy and unproductivity. Excuses make you stationary, immobile and dormant. The goal of an excuse is to provide 'a reason for not doing'. Excuses convince people that those reasons are valid when in truth it keeps them in the same place for a prolonged period of time.

The Power Of Discipline

Developing a life of discipline will help to expunge excuses and encourage you to live with intentionality. In addition, discipline allows you to maximize your potential. In other words, discipline stretches you beyond limitations. A life of discipline will challenge you to abandon the old way of thinking and acting. It has the tendency to push you beyond self-constructed limitations. Instead of fearing success, discipline will cause you to ask yourself questions like, "How far could this gift take me? What more can I do with this gift? How could I use this gift to make people's lives better?" When maximizing your potential, you already know what your potential is, so your goal is now to amplify it. This comes with risk-taking and comfort-zone breaking. Discipline gives you the impetus to exert the necessary time and effort to accomplish your goals. When you have maximized your potential by pushing the boundaries and breaking limitations from your life, then comes the manifestation of your prophecies.

Discipline aids the manifestation of prophecies. A prophetic word spoken over your life without proper employment of discipline will only keep the prophetic word hanging over your head without a chance to find expression in your life. However, when you properly align yourself with the prophecy by developing a life of discipline, the manifestation of your prophecy will take place seamlessly.

One of the common mistakes people have made is that they have tried to 'curate an experience' to supposedly hasten the manifestation of their prophetic word. Most times, this curated experience may cause them to compromise their faith. A popular example of a 'curated experience' in the body of Christ is when a young man or woman receives a word that he/she will get married. Due to the waiting involved in seeing the prophecy fulfilled, he/she then takes a spouse outside of the church with the belief that the spouse will change and become a Christian after marriage. I have seen this happen ever so often, and the turmoil that ensued was almost inescapable. Similarly, we see in Genesis 16 where Sarai out of lack of patience, encouraged her husband to go in unto Hagar so she could conceive in her stead, but this was not the route the Lord had ordained for them. In fact, neither Sarai nor Abram consulted with the Lord before curating this experience. What they knew was that they would have a son but the way they went about seeing it's manifestation was outside of God's plan for them. Though Hagar managed to give birth to a son, he was not the promised son.

> ***" And Sarai said unto Abram, behold now, the Lord hath restrained me from bearing: I pray thee go in unto my maid; it may be that I may obtain***

children by her. And Abram hearkened to the voice of Sarai. And Sarai, Abram's wife took Hagar her maid the Egyptian, after Abram had dwelt ten years in the land of Canaan, and gave her to her husband Abram to be his wife. And he went in unto Hagar, and she conceived: and when she saw that she had conceived, her mistress was despised in her eyes." (Genesis 16:2-4, KJV)

The promise was not given to Hagar, so she could have only produced an Ismael, not an Isaac. Since Isaac was the promised son, he could only come from the womb of Sarai. Many times, the cause of our problems stem from lack of patience.

We should never try to curate an experience to catalyze our prophetic manifestation because our destinies have already been preordained for us and we should not interfere in God's plan. We only need to exercise faith and discipline to see the manifestation of it. There are absolutely no shortcuts to the manifestation of prophecies. God does not need us to find external catalysts to aid our prophetic manifestation. Instead, He requires for us to develop a level of discipline that will partner with the prophetic word over our lives to see it come to pass.

Although discipline comes at a cost, the benefits are definitely rewarding. The cost of discipline includes breaking bad habits but the benefit includes forming new healthy ones. Healthy habits allow you to be in alignment with your goal in a practical way rather than have you foster abstract thoughts that never leave the realm of your mind. It is fair to say that discipline sets people up to get things done in the real world. This is when manifestation happens. You start showing up as the creative that you are which eventually builds resilience. When you have built resilience, people will start noticing you. They will notice your commitment, hunger, discipline and expertise. Now the lights will be on you. There is no going back to the old you. In fact, the old you no longer exist. The old you would have died in chapter 4 of this book, where your isolation led to death and produced humility. The person that is now showing up is confident that he/she has the capacity to dominate and live life intentionally. You will soon discover that your intentionality is your responsibility, and you will also see that the difference between those who constantly win and those who consistently fail is intentionality in what he/she is doing.

When you are intentional, you will go to the extreme to see your dream become a reality. This extreme speaks of your ability to break self-constructed limitations and form healthy habits that will usher you into the greatness that you were created to manifest in the Earth.

I love the posture of Joshua in Exodus 33:11 which tells us that when Moses departed from the presence of the Lord, Joshua stayed back. Joshua had a hunger. He knew what he wanted. Though Moses was his leader, Joshua's actions were not determined by Moses's actions. Moses had several experiences with God; including hearing and speaking to God face to face, but Joshua did not want to live vicariously through his superior, he needed to have these experiences for himself. So when everyone departed, he stayed back to encounter the God of Moses.

> ***" And the Lord spake unto Moses face to face, as a man speaketh unto his friend. And he turned again into the camp: but his servant Joshua, the son of Nun, a young man, departed not out of the tabernacle." (Exodus 33:11, KJV)***

Joshua's desperation for the presence of God may not seem as significant until we see how he grew in spiritual authority to command the sun to stand.

> ***"Then spake Joshua to the Lord in the day when the Lord delivered up the Amorites before the children of Israel, and he said in the sight of Israel, Sun, stand thou still upon Gibeon; and thou, Moon, in the valley of Ajalon. And the sun stood still, and the moon stayed, until the people had avenged***

> ***themselves upon their enemies. Is not this written in the book of Jasher? So the sun stood still in the midst of heaven, and hasted not to go down about a whole day. And there was no day like that before or after it or after it, that the Lord hearkened unto the voice of a man: for the Lord fought for Israel." (Joshua 10:12-14, KJV)***

What Joshua did was tap into a greater level of authority when he spoke to the natural element of the Earth and it obeyed him. However, this one act did not just happen by chance, Joshua learned overtime to tarry in the presence of the Lord.

As you hone your skills and deliver with courage and confidence, your name will begin to spread far and wide. You won't have to audibly promote yourself;

your work will speak for you. Your presence, poise, knowledge and character will amplify who you are. These are qualities that will introduce you to others before you introduce yourself. With all the attention and demand on your gift, it is important that you utilize the spirit of discernment.

As mentioned in a previous chapter, "the path of greatness is not a euphoric path free from problems". As people begin to request your service(s), be careful not to be deceived. The enemy will seize any opportunity to corrupt your gifting if you get distracted (2 Pet 5:8). Be wise enough to know when to say "No". Though you have waited a long time preparing to be announced, be cautious enough to know that not every event you should attend or invitation you should accept. This is why you need the Holy Spirit to give you discerning ears and eyes. Not everything that appears good is necessarily good for you. Remember, you are an instrument of God so allow Him to lead you. Do not be led by your emotions or by your familiarity with people. Be bold enough to turn down an offer without explanation. Saying "No" without an explanation should not be perceived as being rude. There will be times the Holy Spirit will instruct you to turn down an offer without telling you why. Do not be discouraged, there will be more offers coming. When your life aligns with the will of God, it is impossible to fail.

Now, the ball is in your court. What will you do with the knowledge you have acquired? I leave you with this commission, "Go and live an intentional life of greatness. Go! In Jesus' name."

DAILY AFFIRMATIONS

Sunday

Lamentations 3:22-23

Today, the Lord's mercy, compassion and faithfulness abound on my behalf. I am not here by chance; I am here on purpose!

Monday

2 Thessalonians 3:16

Despite how I feel, I will have a peaceful day. I will get up, get dressed and show up. I got this!

Tuesday

Matthew 10:30-31

I am seen and appreciated. Someone is taking notice of the fine details of my life. I know this because the King of kings took the time out to number every strand of hair on my head. I will keep going!

Wednesday

Psalm 46:10

It is midweek and a lot has happened, but I have made it thus far. Therefore, I will Submit all my anxieties to the King, and rest in Him.

Thursday

1 John 5:4

Despite the many challenges and oppositions, I was able to defy the odds and overcome. With God I cannot be defeated.

Friday

Psalm 118:14

I have made it to Friday but not on my own. God has certainly been good. I will continue to draw from his strength. His strength will sustain me!

Saturday

Psalm 23:1

I have been immersed in a never-ending supply of God's provision and I lack nothing. Therefore, I do not need to compare myself to others.

DECLARATIONS

1. I come out of agreement with any covenant that stands against the manifestation of my God-given purpose.
2. I was born to be and do great things.
3. I will respond to the call of God on my life.
4. I refuse to live below my potential.
5. I refuse to be immobile towards God's command.
6. I will push past every self-constructed limitation.
7. I will not accept a mediocre version of myself.
8. I refuse to be discouraged by others' inability to see my vision.

9. I will submit myself to spiritual training to see my vision become reality.

10. I will die empty, and God will be glorified.

NOTES

Made in the USA
Coppell, TX
26 May 2024

32817380R00095